50 World of Curries Recipes for Home

By: Kelly Johnson

Table of Contents

- Indian Butter Chicken Curry
- Thai Green Curry with Chicken
- Malaysian Rendang Beef Curry
- Japanese Katsu Curry
- Sri Lankan Fish Curry
- Jamaican Curry Goat
- Bengali Prawn Curry
- South African Bunny Chow
- Ethiopian Doro Wat
- Persian Ghormeh Sabzi
- Filipino Kare-Kare
- Nepalese Chicken Curry
- Trinidadian Chickpea Curry
- Burmese Coconut Curry
- Moroccan Lamb Tagine
- Vietnamese Yellow Curry
- Laotian Pumpkin Curry
- Afghan Qorma
- Caribbean Vegetable Curry
- British Chicken Tikka Masala
- Iranian Saffron Chicken Curry
- Indonesian Soto Curry
- Singaporean Laksa Curry
- Indian Chana Masala
- Thai Massaman Curry
- Goan Fish Curry
- Indonesian Beef Rendang
- Cambodian Amok Fish Curry
- Pakistani Nihari
- Indian Palak Paneer Curry

- Sri Lankan Dhal Curry
- Mauritian Fish Curry
- Indian Biryani Curry
- Afghan Mutton Korma
- Chinese Curry Beef with Onions
- Iranian Fesenjan (Pomegranate Walnut Curry)
- Indian Aloo Gobi Curry
- Bangladeshi Bhuna Khichuri
- Filipino Bicol Express
- Vietnamese Lemongrass Chicken Curry
- Thai Pineapple Curry
- Indian Lamb Rogan Josh
- Jamaican Pumpkin Curry
- Nepalese Vegetable Curry
- Cambodian Green Curry
- British Vegetable Curry
- Indian Egg Curry (Dimer Jhol)
- Malaysian Fish Head Curry
- Indian Methi Chicken Curry
- Thai Yellow Curry with Tofu

Indian Butter Chicken Curry

Ingredients:

- **For the Marinade:**
    - 500g boneless chicken thighs, cut into bite-sized pieces
    - 1 cup plain yogurt
    - 2 tablespoons lemon juice
    - 2 teaspoons garam masala
    - 1 teaspoon turmeric powder
    - 1 teaspoon chili powder
    - 1 teaspoon ground cumin
    - Salt, to taste
- **For the Curry:**
    - 2 tablespoons butter
    - 1 tablespoon oil
    - 1 large onion, finely chopped
    - 3 cloves garlic, minced
    - 1 tablespoon ginger, minced
    - 2 teaspoons ground coriander
    - 1 teaspoon garam masala
    - 1 teaspoon chili powder
    - 1 can (400g) crushed tomatoes
    - 1 cup heavy cream
    - Salt, to taste
    - Fresh cilantro, for garnish

Instructions:

1. **Marinate the Chicken:**
    - In a bowl, combine yogurt, lemon juice, garam masala, turmeric, chili powder, cumin, and salt. Add the chicken pieces and mix until well coated. Cover and refrigerate for at least 1 hour, or overnight for best results.
2. **Cook the Chicken:**
    - Heat 1 tablespoon of oil and 1 tablespoon of butter in a large skillet over medium heat. Add the marinated chicken (discard excess marinade) and cook until golden brown on all sides, about 6-8 minutes. Remove from the skillet and set aside.
3. **Prepare the Sauce:**

- In the same skillet, add the remaining butter and sauté the chopped onion until soft and golden brown. Add minced garlic and ginger, cooking for another minute until fragrant.
- Stir in coriander, garam masala, and chili powder. Cook for 1-2 minutes, then add crushed tomatoes. Simmer for about 10 minutes until the sauce thickens.

4. **Combine and Finish:**
   - Return the cooked chicken to the skillet, stirring to combine. Pour in the heavy cream and mix well. Simmer for another 5-10 minutes, allowing the flavors to meld. Season with salt to taste.
5. **Serve:**
   - Garnish with fresh cilantro and serve hot with rice or naan bread.

Enjoy your flavorful Indian Butter Chicken Curry!

Thai Green Curry with Chicken

Ingredients:

- **For the Curry:**
    - 500g chicken breast, sliced
    - 1 cup coconut milk
    - 2 tablespoons green curry paste
    - 1 tablespoon fish sauce
    - 1 tablespoon sugar
    - 1 cup mixed vegetables (bell peppers, zucchini, eggplant)
    - Fresh basil leaves, for garnish
    - Cooked jasmine rice, for serving

Instructions:

1. **Cook the Curry:** In a pot, heat a little coconut milk and add the green curry paste. Stir until fragrant. Add the sliced chicken and cook until it turns white. Pour in the remaining coconut milk, fish sauce, and sugar. Stir well. Add the mixed vegetables and simmer for about 10 minutes until cooked through.
2. **Serve:** Garnish with fresh basil leaves and serve hot over jasmine rice.

Malaysian Rendang Beef Curry

Ingredients:

- **For the Curry:**
    - 500g beef, cut into chunks
    - 1 cup coconut milk
    - 2 tablespoons rendang paste (store-bought or homemade)
    - 1 stalk lemongrass, bruised
    - 4 kaffir lime leaves
    - 1 tablespoon tamarind paste
    - 1 tablespoon sugar
    - Salt, to taste

Instructions:

1. **Prepare the Beef:** In a pot, combine the beef, rendang paste, and coconut milk. Bring to a boil. Add the bruised lemongrass, kaffir lime leaves, tamarind paste, and sugar.
2. **Cook the Curry:** Reduce the heat and simmer for 1-2 hours until the beef is tender, stirring occasionally. Season with salt and continue cooking until the sauce thickens.
3. **Serve:** Serve the rendang with steamed rice.

Japanese Katsu Curry

Ingredients:

- **For the Katsu:**
    - 2 pork cutlets (or chicken)
    - Salt and pepper, to taste
    - 1 cup flour
    - 1 egg, beaten
    - 1 cup panko breadcrumbs
    - Oil, for frying
- **For the Curry:**
    - 1 onion, sliced
    - 2 carrots, chopped
    - 2 potatoes, chopped
    - 2 cups chicken stock
    - 2 tablespoons curry powder
    - Cooked rice, for serving

Instructions:

1. **Prepare the Katsu:** Season the pork cutlets with salt and pepper. Dredge in flour, dip in egg, and coat with panko breadcrumbs. Heat oil in a frying pan and fry the cutlets until golden brown and cooked through. Slice and set aside.
2. **Prepare the Curry:** In a separate pot, sauté the sliced onion until soft. Add the carrots and potatoes, cooking for a few minutes. Pour in the chicken stock and curry powder. Simmer until the vegetables are tender.
3. **Serve:** Serve the curry sauce over rice, topped with the sliced katsu.

Enjoy your delicious curries!

Sri Lankan Fish Curry

Ingredients:

- 500g fish fillets (e.g., cod or tilapia)
- 1 onion, chopped
- 2 tomatoes, chopped
- 1 tablespoon curry powder
- 1 teaspoon turmeric powder
- 1 cup coconut milk
- 2 green chilies, slit
- Salt, to taste
- Fresh cilantro, for garnish

Instructions:

1. **Cook the Base:** In a pot, sauté onions until golden. Add tomatoes, curry powder, and turmeric. Cook for a few minutes.
2. **Add Coconut Milk:** Add coconut milk and green chilies, bringing to a simmer.
3. **Add Fish:** Add fish fillets and cook until they are cooked through.
4. **Serve:** Season with salt and garnish with cilantro before serving.

Jamaican Curry Goat

Ingredients:

- 1 kg goat meat, cut into pieces
- 2 tablespoons curry powder
- 1 onion, chopped
- 2 cloves garlic, minced
- 1 ginger piece, grated
- 2 cups water
- 2 sprigs thyme
- 2 potatoes, cubed
- Salt, to taste

Instructions:

1. **Marinate the Goat:** Marinate goat meat with curry powder, salt, onion, garlic, and ginger for at least 1 hour.
2. **Brown the Meat:** In a pot, brown the meat, then add water, thyme, and potatoes.
3. **Simmer:** Simmer until the meat is tender, adding more water if necessary.
4. **Serve:** Adjust seasoning and serve with rice and peas.

Bengali Prawn Curry

Ingredients:

- 500g prawns, cleaned
- 2 tablespoons mustard oil
- 1 onion, finely chopped
- 2 tomatoes, chopped
- 1 teaspoon ginger-garlic paste
- 1 teaspoon turmeric powder
- 1 teaspoon chili powder
- Salt, to taste

Instructions:

1. **Heat the Oil:** Heat mustard oil in a pan. Sauté onions until golden.
2. **Cook the Spices:** Add ginger-garlic paste, turmeric, and chili powder. Cook for a minute.
3. **Add Tomatoes:** Add tomatoes and cook until soft. Add prawns and salt, cooking until prawns are pink.
4. **Serve:** Serve with rice.

South African Bunny Chow

Ingredients:

- 500g curry (lamb, chicken, or vegetarian)
- 4 bread loaves (bunny chow bread)
- Chopped cucumber and carrot, for garnish

Instructions:

1. **Prepare the Curry:** Make your favorite curry (lamb, chicken, or vegetarian).
2. **Hollow the Bread:** Cut the tops off the bread loaves and hollow out the insides to create bowls.
3. **Fill the Bread:** Fill each hollowed loaf with the hot curry.
4. **Serve:** Serve with chopped cucumber and carrot on the side.

Ethiopian Doro Wat

Ingredients:

- 500g chicken pieces (with skin)
- 2 onions, finely chopped
- 2 tablespoons berbere spice mix
- 2 tablespoons butter
- 1 tablespoon ginger-garlic paste
- 1 cup chicken broth
- 4 boiled eggs
- Salt, to taste

Instructions:

1. **Cook Onions:** In a pot, melt butter and cook onions until soft.
2. **Add Spices:** Stir in berbere spice mix and ginger-garlic paste, cooking for a few minutes.
3. **Add Chicken:** Add chicken pieces and broth, simmering until chicken is cooked through.
4. **Add Eggs:** Add boiled eggs to the curry and simmer for a few minutes.
5. **Serve:** Serve with injera or rice.

Persian Ghormeh Sabzi

Ingredients:

- 500g lamb or beef, cubed
- 1 onion, chopped
- 2 cups mixed herbs (parsley, cilantro, fenugreek)
- 1 cup kidney beans, soaked and cooked
- 1 lemon, dried (or juice of 1 lemon)
- 1 teaspoon turmeric
- Salt and pepper, to taste

Instructions:

1. **Sauté Onion:** In a pot, sauté onion until golden. Add meat and turmeric, browning the meat.
2. **Add Herbs:** Add mixed herbs and sauté for a few minutes.
3. **Add Beans and Water:** Add kidney beans and enough water to cover. Add dried lemon and simmer until meat is tender.
4. **Serve:** Season with salt and pepper, serving with rice.

Filipino Kare-Kare

Ingredients:

- 500g oxtail or beef shank, cut into pieces
- 1/2 cup peanut butter
- 1 onion, chopped
- 2 eggplants, sliced
- 1 cup string beans
- 1/2 cup bagoong (fermented shrimp paste)
- 6 cups water
- Salt, to taste

Instructions:

1. **Cook Oxtail:** In a pot, boil oxtail in water until tender.
2. **Sauté Onion:** In another pan, sauté onions, then add peanut butter, mixing well.
3. **Combine:** Add the cooked oxtail and some broth to the peanut mixture.
4. **Add Vegetables:** Add eggplants and string beans, cooking until tender.
5. **Serve:** Serve with bagoong on the side and steamed rice.

Nepalese Chicken Curry

Ingredients:

- 500g chicken, cut into pieces
- 2 onions, finely chopped
- 2 tomatoes, chopped
- 2 tablespoons ginger-garlic paste
- 2 tablespoons curry powder
- 1 cup yogurt
- 1 cup water
- Fresh cilantro, for garnish
- Salt, to taste

Instructions:

1. **Cook Onions:** In a pot, sauté onions until golden brown. Add ginger-garlic paste and cook for a minute.
2. **Add Chicken:** Add chicken pieces, curry powder, and salt, cooking until chicken is browned.
3. **Add Tomatoes and Yogurt:** Add tomatoes and yogurt, simmering for about 15 minutes.
4. **Add Water:** Pour in water and cook until the chicken is tender.
5. **Serve:** Garnish with fresh cilantro and serve with rice.

Trinidadian Chickpea Curry

Ingredients:

- 2 cups canned chickpeas, drained
- 1 onion, chopped
- 2 cloves garlic, minced
- 1 tablespoon curry powder
- 1 teaspoon turmeric
- 1 cup coconut milk
- 1 bell pepper, chopped
- Salt and pepper, to taste

Instructions:

1. **Sauté Onions:** In a pot, heat oil and sauté onions and garlic until fragrant.
2. **Add Spices:** Stir in curry powder and turmeric, cooking for a minute.
3. **Add Chickpeas and Coconut Milk:** Add chickpeas, bell pepper, and coconut milk. Simmer for 10-15 minutes.
4. **Season:** Season with salt and pepper before serving.

Burmese Coconut Curry

Ingredients:

- 500g chicken or pork, cut into pieces
- 2 cups coconut milk
- 2 onions, chopped
- 2 tablespoons curry powder
- 1 tablespoon ginger-garlic paste
- 1 tablespoon fish sauce
- Fresh cilantro, for garnish
- Salt, to taste

Instructions:

1. **Cook Onions:** In a pot, sauté onions until translucent. Add ginger-garlic paste and cook for a minute.
2. **Add Meat:** Add chicken or pork, cooking until browned.
3. **Add Spices and Coconut Milk:** Stir in curry powder, then add coconut milk and fish sauce.
4. **Simmer:** Simmer for about 20-30 minutes until the meat is tender.
5. **Serve:** Garnish with fresh cilantro and serve over rice.

Moroccan Lamb Tagine

Ingredients:

- 500g lamb, cut into chunks
- 1 onion, chopped
- 2 cloves garlic, minced
- 2 tablespoons ras el hanout spice mix
- 1 can (400g) chickpeas, drained
- 1 cup dried apricots, chopped
- 2 cups vegetable broth
- Fresh cilantro, for garnish

Instructions:

1. **Brown the Lamb:** In a tagine or pot, brown the lamb chunks. Remove and set aside.
2. **Cook Onions:** Sauté onions and garlic in the same pot until softened.
3. **Add Spices and Lamb:** Add ras el hanout, chickpeas, apricots, and lamb back to the pot.
4. **Add Broth:** Pour in vegetable broth and simmer for about 1 hour until the lamb is tender.
5. **Serve:** Garnish with fresh cilantro and serve with couscous.

Vietnamese Yellow Curry

Ingredients:

- 500g chicken, cut into pieces
- 2 tablespoons yellow curry powder
- 1 can (400ml) coconut milk
- 2 potatoes, cubed
- 1 onion, sliced
- 1 bell pepper, sliced
- Fresh cilantro, for garnish
- Salt, to taste

Instructions:

1. **Marinate Chicken:** In a bowl, marinate chicken with yellow curry powder and salt for at least 30 minutes.
2. **Cook Onions:** In a pot, sauté onions until soft.
3. **Add Chicken and Coconut Milk:** Add marinated chicken and coconut milk, bringing to a simmer.
4. **Add Vegetables:** Add potatoes and bell pepper, cooking until tender.
5. **Serve:** Garnish with fresh cilantro and serve with rice.

Laotian Pumpkin Curry

Ingredients:

- 500g pumpkin, peeled and cubed
- 1 can (400ml) coconut milk
- 2 tablespoons red curry paste
- 1 cup vegetable broth
- 1 onion, chopped
- Fresh basil, for garnish
- Salt, to taste

Instructions:

1. **Cook Onions:** In a pot, sauté onions until golden.
2. **Add Pumpkin and Curry Paste:** Stir in pumpkin and red curry paste, cooking for a few minutes.
3. **Add Coconut Milk and Broth:** Pour in coconut milk and vegetable broth, simmering until pumpkin is soft.
4. **Serve:** Garnish with fresh basil and serve with rice.

Afghan Qorma

Ingredients:

- 500g lamb or chicken, cut into pieces
- 2 onions, finely chopped
- 2 tablespoons yogurt
- 1 teaspoon turmeric
- 1 tablespoon coriander powder
- 1 cup water
- Fresh cilantro, for garnish
- Salt, to taste

Instructions:

1. **Cook Onions:** In a pot, sauté onions until golden brown.
2. **Add Meat and Spices:** Add lamb or chicken, turmeric, and coriander, cooking until browned.
3. **Add Yogurt and Water:** Stir in yogurt and water, simmering until the meat is tender.
4. **Serve:** Garnish with fresh cilantro and serve with rice.

Caribbean Vegetable Curry

Ingredients:

- 2 cups mixed vegetables (carrots, bell peppers, and peas)
- 1 onion, chopped
- 2 cloves garlic, minced
- 2 tablespoons curry powder
- 1 can (400ml) coconut milk
- 1 cup vegetable broth
- Salt and pepper, to taste
- Fresh cilantro, for garnish

Instructions:

1. **Sauté Onions:** In a pot, sauté onions and garlic until fragrant.
2. **Add Vegetables:** Add mixed vegetables and curry powder, cooking for a few minutes.
3. **Add Coconut Milk and Broth:** Pour in coconut milk and vegetable broth, simmering until the vegetables are tender.
4. **Serve:** Season with salt and pepper, garnish with cilantro, and serve with rice.

British Chicken Tikka Masala

Ingredients:

- 500g chicken breast, cubed
- 1 cup yogurt
- 2 tablespoons tikka masala paste
- 1 onion, chopped
- 2 cloves garlic, minced
- 1 can (400g) chopped tomatoes
- 1 cup cream
- Fresh cilantro, for garnish
- Salt, to taste

Instructions:

1. **Marinate Chicken:** Marinate chicken in yogurt and tikka masala paste for at least 1 hour.
2. **Cook Onions:** In a pan, sauté onions and garlic until soft.
3. **Add Chicken:** Add marinated chicken and cook until browned.
4. **Add Tomatoes and Cream:** Stir in chopped tomatoes and cream, simmering until the chicken is cooked through.
5. **Serve:** Garnish with cilantro and serve with naan or rice.

Iranian Saffron Chicken Curry

Ingredients:

- 500g chicken, cut into pieces
- 1 onion, chopped
- 2 cloves garlic, minced
- 1/4 teaspoon saffron threads, soaked in 2 tablespoons hot water
- 1 teaspoon turmeric
- 1 cup yogurt
- 1 cup chicken broth
- Salt and pepper, to taste

Instructions:

1. **Cook Onions:** In a pot, sauté onions and garlic until golden brown.
2. **Add Chicken and Spices:** Add chicken, turmeric, and saffron with its water, cooking until browned.
3. **Add Yogurt and Broth:** Stir in yogurt and chicken broth, simmering until the chicken is tender.
4. **Serve:** Season with salt and pepper, serving with rice.

Indonesian Soto Curry

Ingredients:

- 500g chicken, cut into pieces
- 2 tablespoons soto spice mix
- 1 onion, chopped
- 2 cloves garlic, minced
- 1 liter chicken broth
- 2 boiled eggs, halved
- Bean sprouts, for garnish
- Fresh cilantro, for garnish
- Lime wedges, for serving

Instructions:

1. **Cook Onions and Garlic:** In a pot, sauté onions and garlic until fragrant.
2. **Add Chicken and Spices:** Add chicken and soto spice mix, cooking for a few minutes.
3. **Add Broth:** Pour in chicken broth and simmer until the chicken is cooked.
4. **Serve:** Ladle into bowls, adding boiled eggs, bean sprouts, and garnishing with cilantro and lime wedges.

Singaporean Laksa Curry

Ingredients:

- 200g rice noodles
- 300g shrimp, peeled and deveined
- 1 can (400ml) coconut milk
- 2 tablespoons laksa paste
- 1 liter chicken broth
- Bean sprouts, for garnish
- Fresh mint, for garnish

Instructions:

1. **Cook Noodles:** Cook rice noodles according to package instructions; set aside.
2. **Cook Shrimp:** In a pot, sauté laksa paste, then add chicken broth and coconut milk. Bring to a simmer.
3. **Add Shrimp:** Add shrimp to the pot, cooking until pink.
4. **Serve:** Divide noodles among bowls, ladle soup over, and garnish with bean sprouts and mint.

Indian Chana Masala

Ingredients:

- 2 cups canned chickpeas, drained
- 1 onion, chopped
- 2 tomatoes, chopped
- 2 tablespoons chana masala spice mix
- 1 teaspoon cumin seeds
- 2 cloves garlic, minced
- Fresh cilantro, for garnish
- Salt, to taste

Instructions:

1. **Cook Onions:** In a pot, heat oil and sauté cumin seeds and onions until golden.
2. **Add Garlic and Tomatoes:** Stir in garlic and tomatoes, cooking until soft.
3. **Add Chickpeas and Spices:** Add chickpeas and chana masala, stirring well.
4. **Simmer:** Add a little water, simmering for 10-15 minutes.
5. **Serve:** Garnish with fresh cilantro and serve with rice or naan.

Thai Massaman Curry

Ingredients:

- 500g beef or chicken, cut into chunks
- 2 tablespoons massaman curry paste
- 1 can (400ml) coconut milk
- 2 potatoes, cubed
- 1 onion, chopped
- 1/4 cup roasted peanuts
- 1 tablespoon tamarind paste
- Fresh cilantro, for garnish

Instructions:

1. **Brown the Meat:** In a pot, brown meat in a little oil.
2. **Cook Onions and Paste:** Add onions and massaman curry paste, cooking for a few minutes.
3. **Add Coconut Milk and Potatoes:** Pour in coconut milk and add potatoes, simmering until the meat and potatoes are tender.
4. **Finish:** Stir in tamarind paste and peanuts before serving.
5. **Serve:** Garnish with fresh cilantro and serve with rice.

Goan Fish Curry

Ingredients:

- 500g fish fillets (such as cod or tilapia)
- 1 onion, finely chopped
- 2 tomatoes, chopped
- 2 tablespoons coconut oil
- 1 can (400ml) coconut milk
- 2 tablespoons Goan curry paste
- Fresh coriander, for garnish
- Salt, to taste

Instructions:

1. **Sauté Onions:** In a pan, heat coconut oil and sauté onions until translucent.
2. **Add Tomatoes and Curry Paste:** Add chopped tomatoes and Goan curry paste, cooking for a few minutes until fragrant.
3. **Add Coconut Milk:** Pour in coconut milk and bring to a simmer.
4. **Add Fish:** Gently add fish fillets, cooking until they are cooked through.
5. **Serve:** Garnish with fresh coriander and serve with rice.

Indonesian Beef Rendang

Ingredients:

- 500g beef, cut into cubes
- 2 tablespoons rendang curry paste
- 1 can (400ml) coconut milk
- 1 onion, chopped
- 2 cloves garlic, minced
- 1 tablespoon tamarind paste
- 1 tablespoon brown sugar
- Fresh cilantro, for garnish
- Salt, to taste

Instructions:

1. **Brown the Beef:** In a pot, brown the beef cubes in a little oil.
2. **Sauté Onions and Garlic:** Add onions and garlic, cooking until soft.
3. **Add Curry Paste and Coconut Milk:** Stir in rendang curry paste and coconut milk, bringing to a simmer.
4. **Add Tamarind and Sugar:** Add tamarind paste and brown sugar, simmering until the beef is tender and the sauce thickens.
5. **Serve:** Garnish with fresh cilantro and serve with rice.

Cambodian Amok Fish Curry

Ingredients:

- 500g fish fillets (such as tilapia or catfish)
- 1 cup coconut milk
- 2 tablespoons amok paste
- 1 banana leaf (for wrapping, optional)
- 1 tablespoon fish sauce
- 1 tablespoon lime juice
- Fresh basil, for garnish

Instructions:

1. **Prepare the Fish:** Cut fish into chunks and set aside.
2. **Mix Ingredients:** In a bowl, mix coconut milk, amok paste, fish sauce, and lime juice.
3. **Combine:** Gently fold in fish chunks.
4. **Wrap in Banana Leaf:** If using, wrap the mixture in banana leaves and steam for about 20 minutes.
5. **Serve:** Garnish with fresh basil and serve with rice.

Pakistani Nihari

Ingredients:

- 500g beef, cut into chunks
- 1 onion, finely sliced
- 2 tablespoons nihari spice mix
- 2 tablespoons ginger-garlic paste
- 1 cup water
- Fresh cilantro, for garnish
- Lemon wedges, for serving

Instructions:

1. **Brown the Meat:** In a pot, heat oil and brown the beef chunks.
2. **Sauté Onions and Spices:** Add onions and ginger-garlic paste, cooking until onions are soft.
3. **Add Water and Spices:** Stir in nihari spice mix and water, simmering until the meat is tender.
4. **Serve:** Garnish with fresh cilantro and serve with lemon wedges and naan.

Indian Palak Paneer Curry

Ingredients:

- 200g paneer, cubed
- 2 cups spinach, blanched
- 1 onion, chopped
- 2 cloves garlic, minced
- 1 tablespoon ginger-garlic paste
- 1 teaspoon garam masala
- 1/2 cup cream
- Salt, to taste

Instructions:

1. **Blend Spinach:** In a blender, puree blanched spinach until smooth.
2. **Sauté Onions and Garlic:** In a pan, sauté onions and garlic until golden.
3. **Add Spinach and Spices:** Stir in spinach puree, ginger-garlic paste, and garam masala, cooking for a few minutes.
4. **Add Paneer and Cream:** Gently add paneer and cream, simmering until heated through.
5. **Serve:** Serve with rice or naan.

Sri Lankan Dhal Curry

Ingredients:

- 1 cup red lentils, rinsed
- 1 onion, chopped
- 2 cloves garlic, minced
- 1 tablespoon curry powder
- 1 can (400ml) coconut milk
- 2 cups water
- Fresh curry leaves (optional)
- Salt, to taste

Instructions:

1. **Sauté Onions and Garlic:** In a pot, heat oil and sauté onions and garlic until fragrant.
2. **Add Lentils and Spices:** Stir in lentils and curry powder, cooking for a minute.
3. **Add Water and Coconut Milk:** Pour in water and coconut milk, simmering until lentils are tender.
4. **Serve:** Season with salt and garnish with fresh curry leaves, if using. Serve with rice.

Mauritian Fish Curry

Ingredients:

- 500g fish fillets (such as snapper)
- 1 onion, chopped
- 2 tomatoes, chopped
- 2 tablespoons curry powder
- 1 can (400ml) coconut milk
- Fresh cilantro, for garnish
- Salt, to taste

Instructions:

1. **Sauté Onions:** In a pan, sauté onions until translucent.
2. **Add Tomatoes and Curry Powder:** Stir in tomatoes and curry powder, cooking for a few minutes.
3. **Add Coconut Milk:** Pour in coconut milk and bring to a simmer.
4. **Add Fish:** Gently add fish fillets, cooking until they are cooked through.
5. **Serve:** Garnish with fresh cilantro and serve with rice.

Indian Biryani Curry

Ingredients:

- 500g basmati rice
- 500g chicken or lamb, cut into pieces
- 1 onion, sliced
- 2 tomatoes, chopped
- 2 tablespoons biryani spice mix
- 1 cup yogurt
- 1/4 cup chopped mint leaves
- 1/4 cup chopped coriander leaves
- 4 cups water
- Salt, to taste

Instructions:

1. **Marinate Meat:** Marinate meat in yogurt and biryani spice mix for at least 1 hour.
2. **Cook Onions:** In a pot, heat oil and sauté sliced onions until golden.
3. **Add Meat and Tomatoes:** Add marinated meat and chopped tomatoes, cooking until meat is browned.
4. **Add Rice and Water:** Stir in rice and water, bringing to a boil. Reduce heat, cover, and simmer until rice is cooked.
5. **Serve:** Garnish with mint and coriander leaves before serving.

Afghan Mutton Korma

Ingredients:

- 500g mutton, cut into pieces
- 2 onions, sliced
- 2 cloves garlic, minced
- 1 tablespoon ginger-garlic paste
- 2 tablespoons korma spice mix
- 1 cup yogurt
- 1/2 cup cream
- Fresh cilantro, for garnish
- Salt, to taste

Instructions:

1. **Brown the Mutton:** In a pot, heat oil and brown the mutton pieces.
2. **Sauté Onions and Garlic:** Add sliced onions and garlic, cooking until soft.
3. **Add Spices and Yogurt:** Stir in ginger-garlic paste, korma spice mix, and yogurt, simmering until mutton is tender.
4. **Finish with Cream:** Add cream before serving, garnishing with fresh cilantro.
5. **Serve:** Serve with naan or rice.

Chinese Curry Beef with Onions

Ingredients:

- 500g beef, thinly sliced
- 1 onion, sliced
- 2 tablespoons curry powder
- 1 tablespoon soy sauce
- 1 cup beef broth
- 2 tablespoons cornstarch mixed with water
- 2 tablespoons vegetable oil
- Salt and pepper, to taste

Instructions:

1. **Marinate Beef:** Marinate sliced beef in soy sauce for 15 minutes.
2. **Stir-fry Beef:** In a pan, heat oil and stir-fry beef until browned.
3. **Add Onions and Curry Powder:** Add onions and curry powder, cooking for a few minutes.
4. **Add Broth:** Pour in beef broth and bring to a simmer.
5. **Thicken Sauce:** Stir in cornstarch mixture until sauce thickens. Serve hot with rice.

Iranian Fesenjan (Pomegranate Walnut Curry)

Ingredients:

- 500g chicken or duck, cut into pieces
- 1 onion, chopped
- 1 cup walnuts, finely ground
- 1/2 cup pomegranate molasses
- 1 cup chicken broth
- 2 tablespoons sugar
- Salt and pepper, to taste

Instructions:

1. **Brown the Meat:** In a pot, heat oil and brown the chicken or duck pieces.
2. **Sauté Onions:** Add chopped onions and cook until soft.
3. **Add Walnuts and Broth:** Stir in ground walnuts, chicken broth, and pomegranate molasses, simmering until meat is tender.
4. **Sweeten and Season:** Add sugar, salt, and pepper, adjusting to taste.
5. **Serve:** Serve with rice.

Indian Aloo Gobi Curry

Ingredients:

- 2 cups cauliflower florets
- 2 potatoes, diced
- 1 onion, chopped
- 2 tomatoes, chopped
- 1 tablespoon ginger-garlic paste
- 1 tablespoon curry powder
- 1/4 teaspoon turmeric
- Fresh cilantro, for garnish
- Salt, to taste

Instructions:

1. **Cook Onions:** In a pot, heat oil and sauté onions until golden.
2. **Add Tomatoes and Spices:** Add tomatoes, ginger-garlic paste, curry powder, and turmeric, cooking until tomatoes soften.
3. **Add Vegetables:** Stir in potatoes and cauliflower, cooking until tender.
4. **Serve:** Season with salt and garnish with fresh cilantro before serving with rice or roti.

Bangladeshi Bhuna Khichuri

Ingredients:

- 1 cup rice
- 1 cup split yellow moong dal
- 500g vegetables (such as peas and carrots)
- 2 onions, sliced
- 1 tablespoon ginger-garlic paste
- 2-3 green chilies
- 1 teaspoon cumin seeds
- 1 teaspoon turmeric
- 4 cups water
- Salt, to taste

Instructions:

1. **Sauté Onions and Spices:** In a pot, heat oil and sauté cumin seeds, then add onions and ginger-garlic paste until golden.
2. **Add Rice and Dal:** Stir in rice, moong dal, turmeric, and vegetables, cooking for a few minutes.
3. **Add Water:** Pour in water and bring to a boil. Reduce heat and simmer until rice and dal are cooked.
4. **Serve:** Season with salt and serve hot.

Filipino Bicol Express

Ingredients:

- 500g pork, sliced
- 1 cup coconut milk
- 2 tablespoons shrimp paste
- 1 onion, chopped
- 3-4 green chilies
- 1 tablespoon ginger, minced
- Salt and pepper, to taste

Instructions:

1. **Cook Pork:** In a pot, sauté pork until browned.
2. **Add Onions and Ginger:** Add onions and ginger, cooking until softened.
3. **Stir in Coconut Milk and Shrimp Paste:** Pour in coconut milk and stir in shrimp paste, simmering until the pork is tender.
4. **Add Chilies:** Add green chilies, cooking for a few more minutes.
5. **Serve:** Season with salt and pepper before serving with rice.

Vietnamese Lemongrass Chicken Curry

Ingredients:

- 500g chicken thighs, cut into pieces
- 2 stalks lemongrass, finely chopped
- 1 onion, chopped
- 2 cloves garlic, minced
- 1 can (400ml) coconut milk
- 1 tablespoon fish sauce
- 1 tablespoon sugar
- 1 tablespoon curry powder
- Fresh cilantro, for garnish
- Salt and pepper, to taste

Instructions:

1. **Sauté Aromatics:** In a pot, heat oil and sauté lemongrass, onion, and garlic until fragrant.
2. **Add Chicken:** Add chicken pieces and cook until browned.
3. **Stir in Coconut Milk:** Pour in coconut milk, fish sauce, sugar, and curry powder, bringing to a simmer.
4. **Cook Until Tender:** Cook until chicken is cooked through and tender.
5. **Serve:** Season with salt and pepper, garnishing with fresh cilantro before serving with rice.

Thai Pineapple Curry

Ingredients:

- 500g chicken or tofu, cut into pieces
- 1 cup pineapple chunks
- 1 onion, sliced
- 1 bell pepper, sliced
- 2 tablespoons red curry paste
- 1 can (400ml) coconut milk
- 2 tablespoons fish sauce (or soy sauce for vegetarian)
- Fresh basil, for garnish

Instructions:

1. **Sauté Vegetables:** In a pan, heat oil and sauté onion and bell pepper until soft.
2. **Add Curry Paste:** Stir in red curry paste, cooking for a minute.
3. **Add Chicken and Pineapple:** Add chicken or tofu and pineapple chunks, cooking until chicken is done.
4. **Add Coconut Milk and Fish Sauce:** Pour in coconut milk and fish sauce, simmering for a few minutes.
5. **Serve:** Garnish with fresh basil and serve with rice.

Indian Lamb Rogan Josh

Ingredients:

- 500g lamb, cut into pieces
- 2 onions, finely chopped
- 2 cloves garlic, minced
- 1 tablespoon ginger, minced
- 2 tablespoons rogan josh spice mix
- 1 cup yogurt
- 1 cup water
- Fresh cilantro, for garnish
- Salt, to taste

Instructions:

1. **Brown the Lamb:** In a pot, heat oil and brown the lamb pieces.
2. **Sauté Onions and Garlic:** Add onions, garlic, and ginger, cooking until soft.
3. **Add Spices and Yogurt:** Stir in rogan josh spice mix and yogurt, cooking until well combined.
4. **Add Water:** Pour in water, simmering until the lamb is tender.
5. **Serve:** Garnish with fresh cilantro and serve with naan or rice.

Jamaican Pumpkin Curry

Ingredients:

- 500g pumpkin, peeled and diced
- 1 onion, chopped
- 2 cloves garlic, minced
- 1 tablespoon Jamaican curry powder
- 1 can (400ml) coconut milk
- 1 bell pepper, sliced
- Fresh thyme, for garnish
- Salt, to taste

Instructions:

1. **Sauté Onions and Garlic:** In a pot, heat oil and sauté onions and garlic until golden.
2. **Add Pumpkin and Curry Powder:** Stir in diced pumpkin and Jamaican curry powder, cooking for a few minutes.
3. **Add Coconut Milk:** Pour in coconut milk and bring to a simmer, cooking until pumpkin is tender.
4. **Add Bell Pepper:** Stir in bell pepper and cook for an additional few minutes.
5. **Serve:** Garnish with fresh thyme and serve with rice.

Nepalese Vegetable Curry

Ingredients:

- 2 cups mixed vegetables (carrots, peas, potatoes)
- 1 onion, chopped
- 2 tomatoes, chopped
- 2 tablespoons curry powder
- 1 can (400ml) coconut milk
- 1 tablespoon ginger-garlic paste
- Fresh cilantro, for garnish
- Salt, to taste

Instructions:

1. **Sauté Onions:** In a pot, heat oil and sauté onions until soft.
2. **Add Tomatoes and Spices:** Stir in chopped tomatoes, ginger-garlic paste, and curry powder, cooking until tomatoes soften.
3. **Add Vegetables:** Add mixed vegetables and coconut milk, simmering until vegetables are tender.
4. **Serve:** Season with salt and garnish with fresh cilantro before serving with rice.

Cambodian Green Curry

Ingredients:

- 500g chicken or tofu, cut into pieces
- 1 cup coconut milk
- 2 tablespoons green curry paste
- 1 bell pepper, sliced
- 1 cup green beans, trimmed
- Fresh basil, for garnish
- Salt, to taste

Instructions:

1. **Cook Chicken or Tofu:** In a pan, heat oil and cook chicken or tofu until browned.
2. **Add Curry Paste:** Stir in green curry paste, cooking for a minute.
3. **Add Coconut Milk and Vegetables:** Pour in coconut milk, adding bell pepper and green beans, simmering until cooked through.
4. **Serve:** Season with salt and garnish with fresh basil before serving with rice.

British Vegetable Curry

Ingredients:

- 2 cups mixed vegetables (carrots, peas, potatoes)
- 1 onion, chopped
- 2 cloves garlic, minced
- 1 tablespoon curry powder
- 1 can (400ml) coconut milk
- 1 tablespoon tomato paste
- Fresh coriander, for garnish
- Salt, to taste

Instructions:

1. **Sauté Onions and Garlic:** In a pot, heat oil and sauté onions and garlic until soft.
2. **Add Spices and Tomato Paste:** Stir in curry powder and tomato paste, cooking for a minute.
3. **Add Vegetables and Coconut Milk:** Add mixed vegetables and coconut milk, simmering until tender.
4. **Serve:** Season with salt and garnish with fresh coriander before serving with rice or bread.

Indian Egg Curry (Dimer Jhol)

Ingredients:

- 6 hard-boiled eggs, peeled
- 2 onions, finely chopped
- 2 tomatoes, chopped
- 1 tablespoon ginger-garlic paste
- 2-3 green chilies, slit
- 1 teaspoon turmeric powder
- 1 tablespoon cumin powder
- 1 tablespoon coriander powder
- 1/2 teaspoon garam masala
- Fresh coriander leaves, for garnish
- Salt, to taste
- 2 tablespoons oil

Instructions:

1. **Sauté Onions:** Heat oil in a pan, add chopped onions, and sauté until golden brown.
2. **Add Tomatoes and Spices:** Stir in ginger-garlic paste, tomatoes, turmeric, cumin, coriander powder, and salt, cooking until tomatoes soften.
3. **Add Eggs:** Gently add boiled eggs, coating them with the masala.
4. **Simmer:** Add a little water if needed, cover, and let it simmer for 5-7 minutes.
5. **Finish:** Sprinkle garam masala and garnish with fresh coriander leaves before serving with rice or bread.

Malaysian Fish Head Curry

Ingredients:

- 1 fish head (preferably from a snapper)
- 2 cups coconut milk
- 1 onion, sliced
- 2 tomatoes, quartered
- 1 tablespoon curry powder
- 1 tablespoon tamarind paste
- 2-3 green chilies, slit
- Fresh curry leaves
- Salt, to taste
- 2 tablespoons oil

Instructions:

1. **Sauté Onions:** Heat oil in a pot, add sliced onions and curry leaves, cooking until fragrant.
2. **Add Curry Powder and Tomatoes:** Stir in curry powder and quartered tomatoes, cooking until tomatoes soften.
3. **Add Fish Head:** Gently add the fish head, tamarind paste, and salt, cooking for a few minutes.
4. **Pour Coconut Milk:** Add coconut milk and bring to a gentle simmer, cooking until the fish is cooked through.
5. **Serve:** Serve hot with rice.

Indian Methi Chicken Curry

Ingredients:

- 500g chicken, cut into pieces
- 1 cup fresh fenugreek leaves (methi), chopped
- 2 onions, finely chopped
- 2 tomatoes, chopped
- 1 tablespoon ginger-garlic paste
- 1 teaspoon turmeric powder
- 1 tablespoon garam masala
- 1 tablespoon cumin seeds
- Salt, to taste
- 2 tablespoons oil

Instructions:

1. **Sauté Onions and Cumin:** Heat oil in a pot, add cumin seeds, and sauté onions until golden.
2. **Add Ginger-Garlic Paste and Tomatoes:** Stir in ginger-garlic paste, chopped tomatoes, turmeric, and salt, cooking until tomatoes soften.
3. **Add Chicken:** Add chicken pieces, cooking until browned.
4. **Add Methi and Simmer:** Stir in chopped fenugreek leaves and garam masala, adding a little water to simmer until chicken is cooked through.
5. **Serve:** Serve with rice or roti.

Thai Yellow Curry with Tofu

Ingredients:

- 400g firm tofu, cubed
- 1 onion, chopped
- 1 bell pepper, sliced
- 2-3 tablespoons yellow curry paste
- 1 can (400ml) coconut milk
- 1 tablespoon soy sauce
- Fresh cilantro, for garnish
- Salt, to taste
- 2 tablespoons vegetable oil

Instructions:

1. **Sauté Onions and Curry Paste:** Heat oil in a pan, add onions, and sauté until soft. Stir in yellow curry paste, cooking for a minute.
2. **Add Tofu and Vegetables:** Gently add cubed tofu and bell pepper, cooking for a few minutes.
3. **Pour Coconut Milk and Soy Sauce:** Add coconut milk and soy sauce, bringing to a simmer.
4. **Cook Until Heated Through:** Cook until heated through and the vegetables are tender.
5. **Serve:** Garnish with fresh cilantro before serving with rice.

www.ingramcontent.com/pod-product-compliance
Lightning Source LLC
LaVergne TN
LVHW081330060526
838201LV00055B/2546